THE TEAM THAT
CHANGED FOOTBALL
FOREVER

UNDERDOGS

SPORTS CHAMPIONS

★ ★ ★

★

★

BY MARTIN GITLIN

45TH PARALLEL PRESS

Published in the United States of America by Cherry Lake Publishing Group
Ann Arbor, Michigan
www.cherrylakepublishing.com

Reading Adviser: Beth Walker Gambro, MS Ed., Reading Consultant, Yorkville, IL
Series Adviser: Virginia Loh-Hagan
Book Designer: Jen Wahi

Photo Credits: cover: Jerry Coli/Dreamstime.com; page 5: © Jerry Coli/Dreamstime.com; page 7: © Jerry Coli/Dreamstime.com; page 9: © New York Jets, Public domain, via Wikimedia Commons; page 13: © Jerry Coli/Dreamstime.com; page 15: © Jerry Coli/Dreamstime.com; page 17: © Bill Young/San Francisco Chronicle via AP; page 19: © AP Photo/Al Messerschmidt; page 23: © Tony Tomsic via AP; page 27: © Tony Tomsic via AP

45th Parallel Press is an imprint of Cherry Lake Publishing Group.

Library of Congress Cataloging-in-Publication Data

Names: Gitlin, Martin, author.
Title: The team that changed football forever / Martin Gitlin.
Description: Ann Arbor : 45th Parallel Press, 2023. | Series: Underdogs:
    sports champions | Audience: Grades 4-6 | Summary: "The Team that
    Changed Football Forever takes readers inside the 1969 Super Bowl game
    between the Baltimore Colts and the New York Jets. Provides background
    leading up to the game, review of the game, why the world was shocked,
    and what happened afterward. From players no one believed in to teams no
    one thought could win, Underdogs: Sports Champions covers some of
    history's greatest underdogs. Written in a strong narrative nonfiction
    style, the storytelling in these books will captivate readers. The
    series includes considerate vocabulary, engaging content, clear text and
    formatting, and compelling photos. Educational sidebars include extra
    fun facts and information"-- Provided by publisher.
Identifiers: LCCN 2023005889 | ISBN 9781668927793 (hardcover) | ISBN
    9781668928844 (paperback) | ISBN 9781668930311 (ebook) | ISBN
    9781668931790 (pdf)
Subjects: LCSH: New York Jets (Football team)--History--Juvenile
    literature. | Super Bowl (3rd : 1969 : Miami, Fla.)--Juvenile
    literature.
Classification: LCC GV956.N37 G | DDC 796.332/6407471--dc23/eng/20230214
LC record available at https://lccn.loc.gov/2023005889

Cherry Lake Publishing would like to acknowledge the work of the Partnership for 21st Century Learning, a network of Battelle for Kids. Please visit http://www.battelleforkids.org/networks/p21 for more information.

Note from publisher: Websites change regularly, and their future contents are outside of our control. Supervise children when conducting any recommended online searches for extended learning opportunities.

Printed in the United States of America
Corporate Graphics

TABLE OF CONTENTS

Introduction

What makes sports fun? Fans love watching sports. They love watching great athletes. They love seeing the best in action. They're awed by their skills. They're awed by their talent.

But what makes sports interesting? One never knows what will happen. Fans can expect an outcome. Their side could win. Or their side could lose. Nobody knows for sure.

Sometimes an upset happens. This is when a team that's expected to win loses. Upsets make fans sad. They confuse people.

Sometimes an underdog rises to the top. Underdogs can be players. They can be teams. They have little chance of winning. Yet, they win.

Teammates congratulate Joe Namath on a touchdown.

Surprises happen. They're shocking. But they're wonderful. They're fun to watch.

That's why games are played. That's why fans watch games. They don't know who's going to win. They don't know who's going to lose. This is the point of sports. Not knowing is exciting.

Upsets in sports are legends. Legends are great stories. They're remembered forever. Underdogs make people smile. They inspire. They give hope. There are many sports champions. The most loved are underdogs. This series is about them.

Namath's confidence in his team set the tone for the 1968 New York Jets' winning season.

Warming Up

The year was 1964. The date was November 28. It was a Saturday. Thanksgiving had come and gone. Turkey had been eaten. Football would be played the next day. Fans could just focus on football.

Fans were also excited about 2 off-field events. The National Football League (NFL) was holding its draft. A draft is when teams select the best college players. The NFL hopes to build their team. They hope to sign players to contracts. The American Football League (AFL) is the NFL's rival. They were also hosting a draft.

Most players want to be in the NFL. They believe it's better. It has been around much longer. But one superstar didn't care which league. He wanted to go to the highest bidder. His name is Joe Namath. Namath went to the

Joe Namath at the beginning of his career in 1965. This photo was taken after he'd signed with the New York Jets.

University of Alabama. He was a quarterback. Quarterbacks are the most important players. They call the plays. They're like the team captain. They handle the ball. They throw the ball. They run the entire offense. Playing offense means playing to score.

The St. Louis Cardinals are an NFL team. They drafted Namath. The New York Jets are an AFL team. They also drafted Namath. The Jets offered him twice as much money. Namath chose the Jets. The Jets never regretted the decision. Neither did Namath. They grew together.

Three years later, they were ready. They were headed for greatness. Namath led them to the playoffs. Playoffs are final games. They determine the champion. The Jets played against the Oakland Raiders. They played for the AFL title. Title means championship.

Millions of fans watched. Fans went to the games. They also watched on TV. They were in for a shock. The Raiders had the lead. This happened late in the game. Then suddenly, TV watchers got confused. The game got tuned out.

Joe Namath joined the Jets. And he changed football. It had been more of a ground game. Quarterbacks most often handed off the ball. They gave it to running backs. Running backs carry the ball. They do running plays. But Namath had a powerful arm. Weeb Ewbank was the Jets' coach. He loved to see Namath throw. And that is what Namath did. He led the AFL with 3,379 yards passing. This happened in 1966. Namath was just warming up. He threw more than 4,000 yards. This happened in 1967. Namath was the first quarterback to reach that total. He also tossed 26 touchdown passes that year. But he had 2 problems. One was knee injuries. The other was interceptions. Interceptions are bad passes. These passes were caught by the other team. Namath had 27 in 1966. He had 28 in 1967. He led the AFL in interceptions both seasons.

The TV station played a children's movie. The movie was called *Heidi*.

Fans were mad. They missed seeing Namath play hero. Namath had passed. This led to the winning touchdown. The Jets became league champions.

The Super Bowl is the NFL championship game. It's played every year. The Jets played against the Baltimore Colts. Few thought the Jets could win. The Colts were powerful. They had lost only once all year.

One man believed the Jets could beat the Colts. And he said so. That man was Namath. Most fans just laughed at him. Soon they would not be laughing.

Don Maynard leaps for a catch during the 1968 "Heidi Game" against the Oakland Raiders.

The Upset

The Super Bowl is played on Sunday. In 1969, it was to be played in Miami. Miami is in Florida. It was January 9, 1969. That was the Thursday before the Super Bowl. The Touchdown Club hosted a dinner. Joe Namath was one of the speakers.

He arrived at the podium. Podiums are speaking posts. He didn't have time to say a word. A Colts fan was in the room. He beat him to it. He yelled the Colts were going to destroy the Jets. Namath had a quick answer. He said, "Whoa there, buddy. I got news for you. We're going to win the game. I guarantee it."

His words made big news. Few thought the Colts could lose. Fans favored them to win by 18 points. Most people joked about Namath's words. They had a reason for that. The NFL was thought to be a much better league.

Don Shula, coach of the 1968 Baltimore Colts. They were expected to win easily against the Jets.

The first 2 Super Bowls proved it. The Green Bay Packers had won both. They had easily beaten the AFL champions.

Many felt that the Colts were better than the Packers. The Colts had a record of 13–1 that year. The Jets had lost 3 games. And most thought they played against worse teams.

The numbers didn't add up to a Jets victory. Namath was a great quarterback. But the Colts had an incredible defense. Playing defense means protecting the end zone. The Colts allowed the fewest points in the NFL. They gave up an amazing average of just 10 points per game. It was hard to score against them.

And they were on a roll. The Colts destroyed the Cleveland Browns. They won the league crown. They won that game 34–0. The Jets barely beat the Raiders to reach the Super Bowl.

Sunday finally arrived. The teams were ready. Fans across the country turned on their TV sets. Nearly everyone expected the Colts to win. They got a stunning surprise.

★ Joe Namath makes a throw while Dave Herman (67) holds off the opposition.

The Shocker

Something was different. The 1969 Super Bowl was not going as expected. Fans at the game saw that from the start. So did the millions watching it on TV. The Jets' defense was shutting down the Colts' offense. The Colts had chances to score. They missed a field goal. Field goals are kicks through the goalposts. They're worth 3 points. They fell on a Jets fumble. They had the ball. The ball was 6 yards from a touchdown. But the Jets stole a pass. They stopped the drive.

Namath picked up his game. So did his running back. Matt Snell was the running back. He caught a pass for 12 yards. He ran the ball for 5 yards. Then he scored a touchdown. The Jets led 7–0.

Fans were stunned. They could hardly believe it. The second half began. The Colts couldn't move the ball at all.

Quarterback Joe Namath picks up his game to help his team get their first touchdown of Super Bowl III against the Baltimore Colts.

But the Jets did. Namath and Snell kept it up. Namath threw a 14-yard pass. He threw it to George Sauer. He tossed an 11-yard pass. He tossed it to Pete Lammons. He fired a 14-yarder to Snell. Soon Jim Turner kicked a field goal. New York stretched its lead to 13–0.

The clock was ticking. The Colts were running out of time. Namath threw a long pass to Sauer. He set up another field goal. Now the score was 16–0.

The Colts were desperate. Don Shula was the Coach. He changed quarterbacks. He put in Johnny Unitas. Unitas was a top player. He was famous. He drove the Colts downfield. The Colts made a touchdown. But it didn't matter. It was too late. The Jets had 16 points. The Colts had 7 points.

Namath was true to his word. The Jets had won. They shocked the football world. But they had done more than that. They had quieted critics of the AFL. The AFL had been around since 1960. And now folks knew their teams could play great football. Namath and the Jets had proved it.

SAME SPORT, DIFFERENT STORY

★
★

It was 1972. The Miami Dolphins set a record. They didn't lose a game that season. Nobody in NFL history had ever done that. The Miami Dolphins were the first. They wanted to keep it that way. In 2008, they got nervous. The 2008 Super Bowl had begun. The New England Patriots were close to winning. They had a 16–0 record. They were playing the New York Giants. The Patriots were favored to win. They would be champions. They would also join the Miami Dolphins. They, too, would have a no-loss season. The Patriots seemed to have no flaws. Tom Brady was perhaps the greatest quarterback ever. They scored 37 points per game. They had one of the best defenses. They led 14–10. Time was running out. But the Giants marched downfield. Their quarterback was Eli Manning. He fired a pass to Plaxico Burress. The Giants made a touchdown. They had taken the lead. There were only 35 seconds left. Soon it was over. The Patriots had lost. They didn't break any records. The 1972 Dolphins were relieved.

The Response

The Jets were celebrating their victory. A reporter went up to Joe Namath. He wanted him to talk about his greatness. But Namath didn't wish to praise himself.

The reporter said, "You're king of the hill."

Namath said, "No, no. We're king of the hill. We got the team, brother!"

Yes, they did. His team had pulled off the biggest upset in NFL history. And Namath was right. It was a team effort.

Namath didn't throw a touchdown pass. He never even passed in the fourth quarter. The hero was Matt Snell. He rushed for 121 yards. He would never again reach that total. He caught 4 passes for 40 yards. And he scored 2 touchdowns. He had a great season.

Matt Snell (41) pushes his way down the field during Super Bowl III. He was the hero of the game.

Winston Hill was an offensive lineman. Linemen are players who block. They open holes for running backs. They also protect quarterbacks. He said, "Snell is a great runner. He doesn't ask for much room." Snell made do with what was available.

Of the game, Hill said, "I knew we could do it. We ran against the best teams in our league. What's so special about the Colts?"

There were many heroes on defense. The entire unit was strong. They shut down the powerful Colts. They stole the ball from them 5 times. Four of them were interceptions.

Larry Grantham was a Jets linebacker. Linebackers stop the offense. Grantham said he had a feeling before the game. He said, "All week long all you read about was Joe Namath against the great Baltimore defense. Nobody wrote anything about our defense. But we felt we had a chance to shut them out."

Nobody but the Jets felt that way. But it didn't matter. They didn't need anyone else to believe in them. That confidence had carried them to victory.

★ Joe Namath had dropped out of the University of Alabama. He did this to play football. More than 40 years later, he went back. He graduated in 2007. He was 64 years old. He said, "It was fun. But it was hard." He said it was hard making time to study.

★ Namath was called "Broadway Joe." He acted on stage. He did ads. He also appeared in TV and movies. He even had his own TV show. It was called *The Joe Namath Show*.

★ Namath became a fashion star. In the 1970s, he wore a fur coat and sunglasses. He did this at games. He also wore fur coats to nightclubs. He liked dressing up. He often wore flashy clothes.

★ Namath wrote a book. The book is about his life. It's called *All the Way: My Life in Four Quarters*.

Moving On

Football history was made in 1970. That is when the NFL and AFL merged. They joined together. They formed one league. The merge started in 1966. The first Super Bowl was also being planned. The AFL and NFL champions first met in 1967.

Some believe the merger resulted from the 1969 Super Bowl. They think it was spurred by the Jets winning. But that's not true. It was created 3 years earlier. But the New York victory was important. Many NFL fans did not want the leagues to come together. The Jets proved that the AFL was strong.

That was shown again a year later. The Kansas City Chiefs won the next Super Bowl. The Chiefs were AFL champions. They beat the Minnesota Vikings. The Vikings

Joe Namath throws a pass during Super Bowl III. After this game, Namath became the most famous athlete in the United States.

had won the NFL title. They were favored to win. But the Chiefs beat them badly.

By that time, Namath became a superstar. He was perhaps the most famous athlete in America.

The NFL had better quarterbacks. But Namath had the power of personality. He showed it. He boldly stated his Jets would upset the Colts. It remains one of the biggest shockers in sports history.

The Pro Football Hall of Fame is a big honor. Joe Namath was invited to be inducted. Inducted means to be added as a member. He made it in 1985. That was 8 years after he retired from football. Some critics feel he did not deserve the honor. Some think he was only chosen only because he won the 1969 Super Bowl. It's a valid idea. Namath didn't have great numbers. He threw far more interceptions than touchdowns. His teams won 62 games when he played. They lost 63. But others feel he belongs in the Hall of Fame. They point out that Namath had knee injuries. That stopped him from realizing his greatness. That is also true. Namath missed many games because of knee problems. He only played 2 full seasons after 1968.

Learn More

Books

Doeden, Matt. Coming Up Clutch: *The Greatest Upsets, Comebacks, and Finishes in Sports History*. Minneapolis, MN: Millbrook Press, 2018.

Peters, Mark. *The Ultimate Joe Namath Fun Fact and Trivia Book*. Lewisville, TX: Perfect World Marketing, 2013.

Zweig, Eric. *It's a Numbers Game! Football*. Boone, IA: National Geographic Kids, 2022.

Explore These Online Sources with an Adult:

Britannica Kids: National Football League

Gen Jets – New York Jets Kids Club

Sports Illustrated Kids: NFL Zone

Glossary

defense (DEE-fens) Playing to defend the goal or keep the other team from scoring

draft (DRAFT) An event during which NFL teams select top college players

field goal (FEELD GOHL) A kick through the goal posts worth 3 points

inducted (in-DUHK-tid) To be added as a member

interception (in-ter-SEP-shuhn) A pass usually thrown by a quarterback caught by the opposing team

legend (LEH-juhnd) An extremely famous story that is told many times

linebacker (LYNE-bak-er) A leader of the defense whose job is to stop the offense's running attack

lineman (LYNE-muhn) A player who blocks opposing players to open holes for running backs to run through or protect the quarterback

merger (MURJD) Two leagues came together to form one league

offense (AW-fens) Playing to score

playoffs (PLAY-awfs) Games played to determine an overall champion

podium (POH-dee-uhm) Speaking post

quarterback (KWOR-ter-bak) A player on a football team responsible for calling the plays, throwing the ball, and running the offense

Super Bowl (SOO-puhr BOWL) The ultimate championship game in the NFL

title (TYE-tuhl) a championship win

underdog (UHN-der-dawg) A player or team that has little chance of winning but ends up winning

upset (UHP-set) When the team that is expected to win loses

Index

About the Author

Martin Gitlin is a sports book author based in Cleveland. He won more than 45 awards as a newspaper sportswriter from 1991 to 2002. He covered the NFL Cleveland Browns for more than 20 years. Marty has had more than 200 books published since 2006. Most were written for students.